HOLA FITNESS

Poetry Inspiration in the Gym

by Uncle John

Table of Contents – POEMS

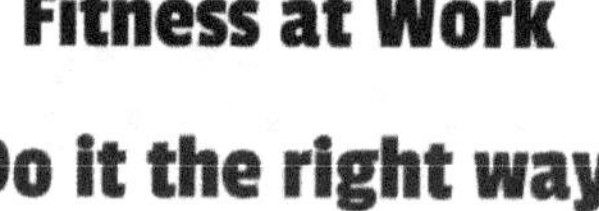

1 - Hola

Hola maiden how beautiful

I like what you do with your hair

The way you transform the air

Walking in rhythm to your heart aware

Balance in motion

On a path and a woke

Bright-eyed smiles

Like kind kinfolk

Look to the sky

Changes near and far

Look at your way of training

Amazed at who you are

Gaze on you like a star in the night

Brilliant work illuminates the hours

Inspiration absorbs the light

Love vibrates you can feel its powers

2 - Focus on Fitness

Enfoque en el Aptitud

Weight training

Watch your composure

Follow your movement

Breathe and do over

Measured time

Walking with quickness

Challenging and gratifying

Focus on fitness

Consistent

Balanced

Buoyant

Physical inspiration

Athletic

Esthetic

Poetic

Energetic

3 – Star Trail

Estela de las Estrellas

A flash of light in the dark night

Captures my attention and view

Feeling energized animated awake

The star trail everyday is new

Ready to run

To tame the wild spirit

Climb the stars higher

In a musical world to hear it

I want to be in this company

Hands move in harmony

The way she parts her hair to see

She is strong & dances on one knee

The star is light

Energy in reflection

Stars are an inspiration

To look at with admiration

4 – Inspiration

Inspiracion

Stellar inspiration
Changes transformation
For the writer she is a muse
Aesthetic like a sky of golden hues

Like the butterfly she is tender
She is strong and does not pretend
Like birds and bees
Moves fast like a refreshing breeze

She listens as she works at night
Brings inspiration in sight
Radiates warmth & luminous beauty
To open the morning light

Hola good morning

Glad to greet you

Welcome in

Thanks come again

5 – Garden of Fitness

Jardin de Aptitud

To be happy and fit

We work on it

Joy in the fitness garden

Embodies the integrity of creation

Authentic and meaningful moments

Turn work into energy and sensation

Endearing dancing butterflies
Stellar spirit gym gems
Guide by the mirror of change
Wings of strength to sustain them

Genuine attentive butterfly
Rallying inspiration
Earthy
Lovely angelic location

Love is like a butterfly
Exquisite and so elusive
To hold in your hand and heart
Love that is inclusive

6 - Dancing Butterflies

Mariposas Bailando

Meet in a place of vigorous training
Sun in our hearts never raining
Move our bodies up down and turning
There is much to be learning

The environment supports our routine
Building health we do the same scene
Every day is different and new
Work on challenges breaking through

There is a start to brighten the day
After working out the night
Dancing butterflies are in the gym
Make me smile and feel alright

The body has hidden treasure few find
The gym provides the space and time
Proper mood in our frame of mind
Adjust as we pull lift walk & climb

GYM

7 – Cardio Fitness Aerobic Health

Gym Workout

Aptitud Cardio Salud Aerobica

Leg lifts & stretches

Split squat sketches

Pallof press

Hand to chest

Seated row with cable bands
Overhead press dumbbell hands
Goblet squat
Dumbbell deadlift now what

Improve my gait
Kettleball & suitcase carry
Balance posture
Walk climb steps primary

Enthusiasm
Motivation
Movement
Core-strength

8 - Elusive Star

Estrella Esquiva

Elusive Star Bright

Telepathic trail leads to light

Hard work blooming beauty

Share the best I can write

Time has a story to tell
Genuine without romance
On the way wish you the best
To love you show you dance

Who is not as strong as you
Dances all night on a dance floor
Your elegant steps capture attention
Birds bees butterflies soar

Sunflower blooms butterfly light
Elusive to catch spreads beauty
Birds singing in the air
Bees working to do duty

9 – The Buzz & The Butterfly

El Zumbido y las Mariposas

Come with me we can make honey
Bee tells butterfly & she laughs
You've been chasing my tail all day
Follow movement with choreographs

Bee sees two butterflies
A beautiful twin for bee with interest
He notices the mirror & two are one
She winks & bee sees he is different

Bee asks can I train to fly like you
Graceful strong balanced true
Show me flowers we enjoy too
You have wings & a way about you

Hear the buzz and know who you are
Bee answers you be the butterfly star
She says stay on my radar
We will meet again near and far

10 – Stella New

Estela Nueva

Gym workout is not easy
Build on routine effort & suitability
Find harmony
Work heartily

To learn observably
Ingeniously
By the way
You are glowing

You shine tirelessly
Notably
Vibrantly
With stamina

Stella new
Wake gleefully
Inspiration and hair do
Smile about you

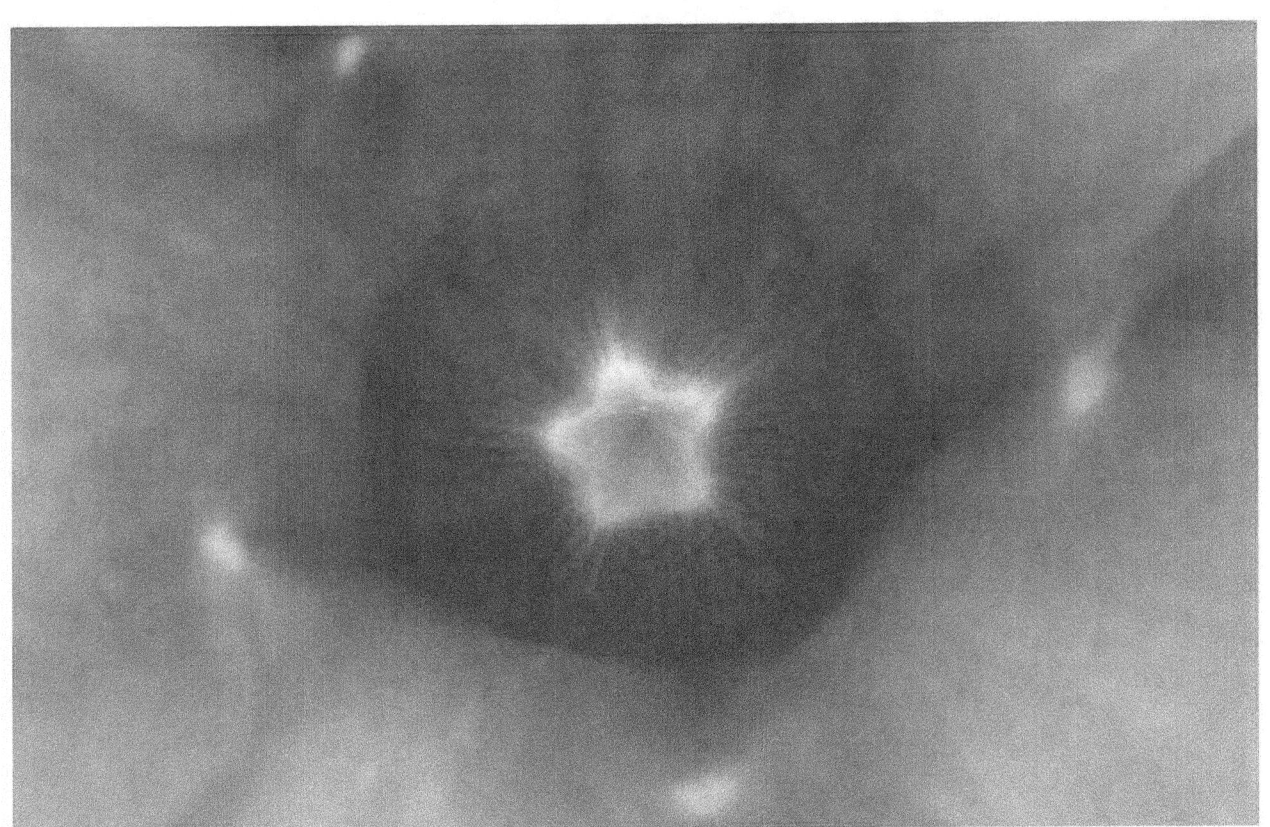

11 – STAR

Estrella

I would be lost without God
Thank the Lord I found you
True to your heart you are
One eye on my mind the star

Who shows the way
Starts the day
Moves the mountains in our mind
See the star build wellness in time

May this heart be changed renewed
With light I see flowing in you
Shining star in place
Stellar illumination with grace

There you are in the distance
Shining with love and persistence
Full of light and power from afar
Wisdom & strength you are the star

12 – Butterfly Posture

Postura de la Mariposa

Women are stronger in endurance
Training smarter with intuition
The company they keep
Always try to stay in good condition

Every day I can I greet her star trail
Train in pain and then prevail
Exercise & health a true treasure
A measure of work and leisure

Follow the light in the mirror window
Look at her butterfly pose
Feel your eyes open the world
Lovely to perceive as a beautiful rose

You are a model in what you do
To know the best of you
Durable delicate special prowess
Creativity nourishes bright progress

13 – Ambience & Inspiration

Ambiente e Inspiracion

**Bounce the way you move
See you develop and improve
In the gym atmosphere
Your focus is always here**

Grateful every time I see
The way she motivates me
Deep connection in reflection
Wonder who is she

Guiding amicable blossoming
Reading insightful
Encouraging
Learning atmosphere

Esteemed
Self-confident talent
Enthusiastic lively awesome
Genial

14 – Spring

Primavera

The way you put spring in the air
I feel the way you move your hair
The color of the clothes you wear
The way you ignore makes me share

I searched the world for a girl like you
I found a four leaf clover too
Look up discover self-love you are
With renewed strength you are a star

The way you are
When you hold the floor
The look in your eyes
Makes my heart soar

Feelings wait and then forget
The wet sweat for what we get
Spring you put in your step
Makes you full of pep

15 - Hola Strawberry Moon

Hola Luna de Fresa

Summer begins like the day
Happy hello Strawberry Moon
Brilliance and wisdom say
Reflection on health in tune

Let there be light
In my mind to write
Continue to the heart of the star
Mysterious inner circle you are

A strong foundation & connection
Enriching inspiring delightful dance
Love beautiful exercise
Activity and self-acceptance

You the adventurer gladden
With excitement about to happen
Heart berry moon abundance passion
Explore the best in new horizons

16 – Starlight

Estrella Brillante

Beauty of a star shining dearly
Light reaches us clearly
Dancer in sight near me
Feeling joy sincerely

Gym achievements bring respect
Integrity equality lively action
Energy strength transformative effect
Light attention

Everytime you train
With full consideration
All routine is different new
Devotion and dedication

Brilliant star within the glow
Resplendent and radiant like a show
Who you are
A shining star

17 – Morning Star

Lucero del Alba

Bright and morning star
Looks like you're having fun
But they don't call this a fun-out
You love to work out

You let your hair down
Rays of light in all directions
Penetrating distance eyes glisten
You silence the world to listen

And the way you make me laugh
So I can stretch like a giraffe
The way you pull on those rings
I see where you hide your wings

Your health is your wealth
That star is our sun
This star recreates herself in the gym
The dancers raise their limbs

18 – Butterfly Exercise

Ejercicio de Mariposa

Butterfly run butterfly climb
Butterfly dancing plays in my mind
Good feeling dancer shows
Butterfly awake dawn glows

Hope then transformation
Gym stamina an inspiration
Enthusiasm brings motivation
Experiences with live sensations

Butterfly eyes butterfly exercise
Be healthy happy solvent & wise
Listen & feel your heart beat love
Your smile soars with spirit above

She has four wings free to flutter & fly
She is like a beautiful flower in the sky
Comes out at night & greets the day
Butterfly exercise can teach ballet

19 – When the Sun Shines Bright

Cuando el Sol Brilla

You move me at night
Like the fresh air
When the sun shines bright
You make me aware

You are here in my mind
When I look for you in my dream
You put a light in my heart
And teach me to breathe

You are positive spirit
In a bird of happiness nest
Beautiful butterfly in sight
You bring out the best

Sun star in our life
You are far away and so loved
We start to feel hot
As you get closer with the light up

20 The Deck of Destiny

La Cubierta del Destino

Gracious divine graceful and true
Eyes are like windows & mirrors too
Mysterious adventurous adaptive
Encouraging exciting energetic active

Look the star of destiny
Gazing at butterfly who you are see
The beauty of what you do
Comes from inside the roses in you

Fortune stellar full of spirit
Water sun and earth near it
Wings of strength to endure it
The heart beats love you can hear it

Siblings exceptional are special
Dancers choreograph what I see
Magical inevitable twisted heavenly
This is the deck of destiny

21 - Reflections in the Mirror

Reflejos en el Espejo

Love is eternal
Springs from the spirit
Opens the heart
In rhythm to hear it

Reflections in the mirror
Movements are clearer
Stretching limbs & hair swaying
Magnificent work is playing

Calm and confident
Motivation and concentration
Patient and persistent
Encouraged and competent

My heart beats merrily in song

To a star shining dear

Some nights far away like Milky Way

Feelings come when her light is near

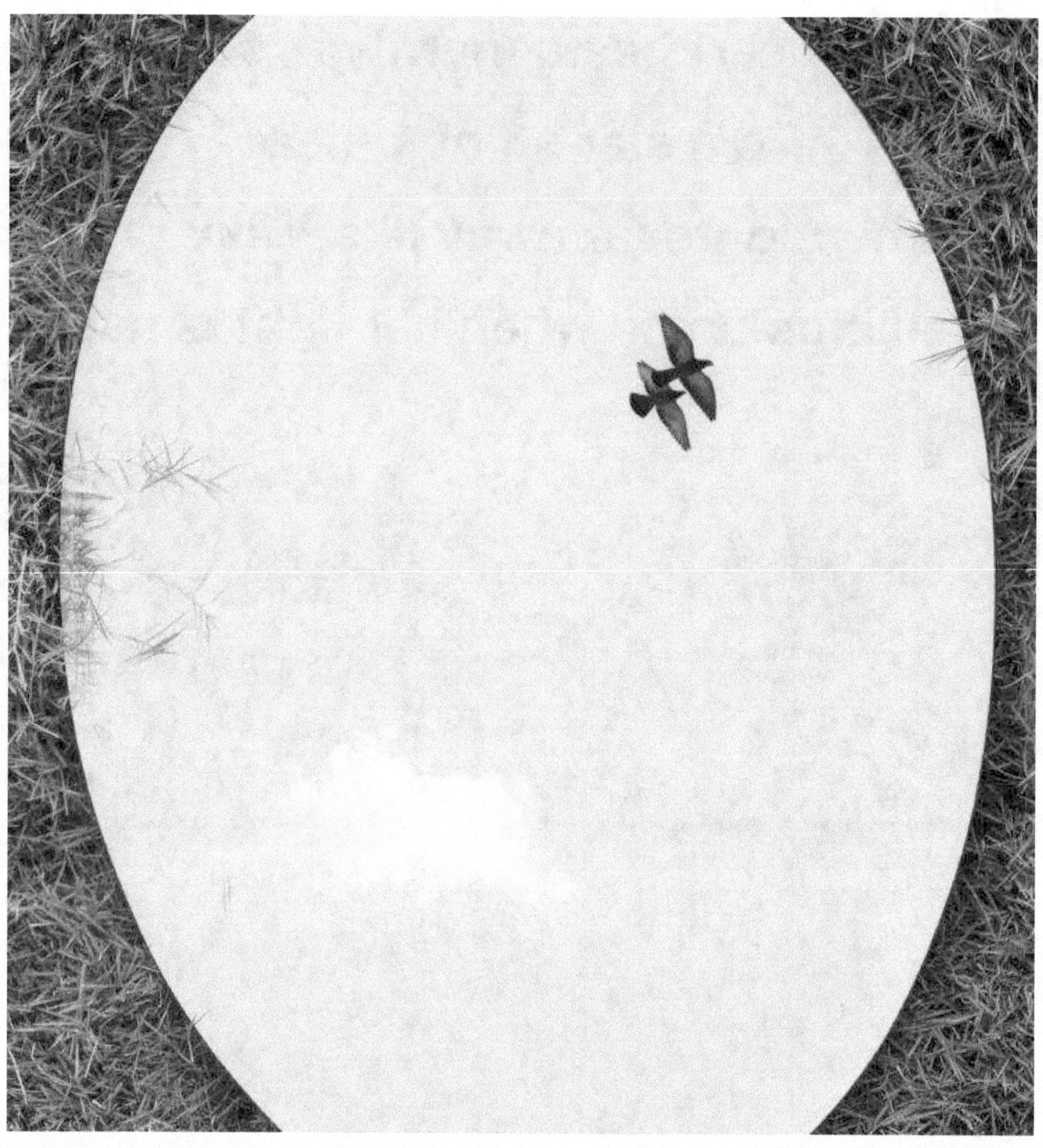

22 – Butterfly Fitness

Aptitud de la Mariposa

Work out a plan and routine
Hydrate stretch feel like a queen
Toss your head girl to the beat
Hula your hips & shake your feet

Do cartwheels in the fall
In the stretch room playing ball
Twinkle fingers listen in your ears
Never felt better in all your years

You know how to pause and pace
Butterfly fitness in a happy face
Follow the direction shown
Stay in the judgment free zone

Work consistent positive resilience
Strong energy overcomes resistance
Marigolds brighten up the cloudy way
Workout clears mind for nicer day

23 – Wake of the Stars

Despertar de las Estrellas

Wake of the stars
Look above
Venus rises
Greet morning workout with love

Your future is in the mirror
Love that can last
Present reflects its charm
A physical training enthusiast

The first is the strongest
Last is the fastest
Comes like a night comet
Tail running towards us

Look for sky signs work on Smith bars
Wake of the stars
See your smile hear your laugh
It´s very bright in a photograph

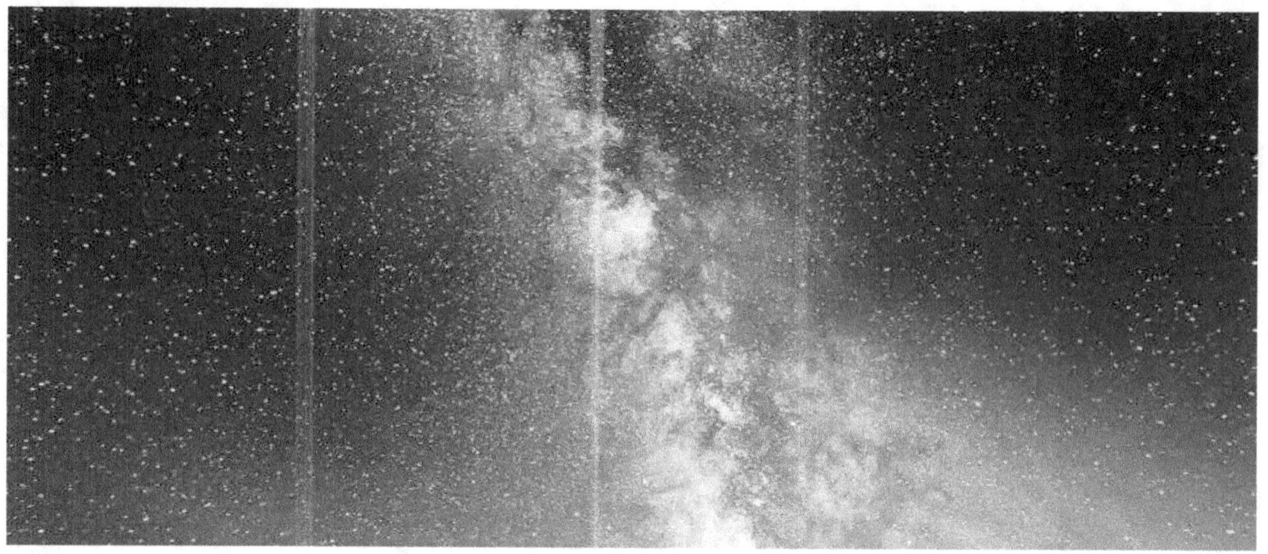

24 – Stella Shine

Brillo Estela

Stella shine
Far away in my mind
Shimmer with the night awake
Until your light finds

The gold star is coming
She looks like a newbie
She moves me with a question
She is so carefree

Like the tail of a comet`s
Trail at night
Following every detail
She is a delight

She is like the song
Playing in my ears
Inside a dream
Of a thousand years

Space & Webb Telescope Pictures

courtesy, **NASA**

& Space Telescope Science Institute

Uncle John´s Hands

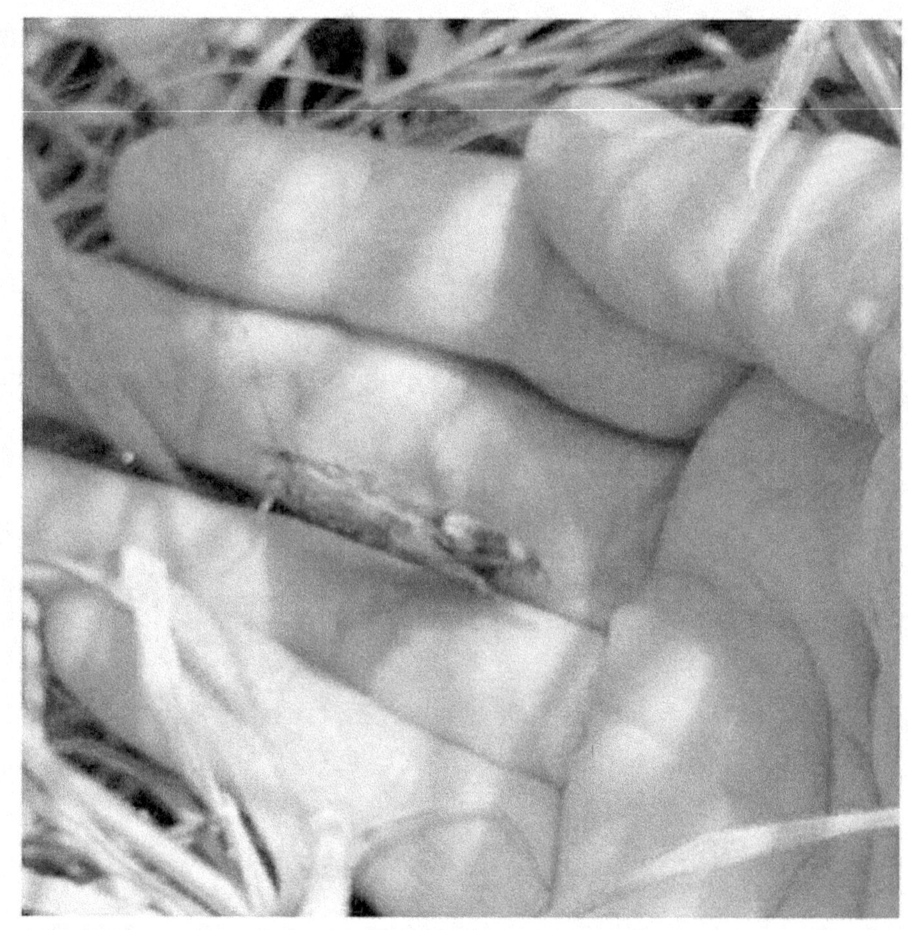

San Francisco

Golden Gate Park

San Francisco

California Academy of Sciences

Hola Fitness

First Edition December 24, 2024

© 2024 Interstarnet.llc

BOOK PUBLISHER

INTERSTARNET

548 Market St. PMB 885488

San Francisco, CA. 94104

2024 - 2025 Publishing

Poetry Books by Uncle John

Web Development Company

WEB.catering

Books1st@gmail.com

INTERSTARNET
Book Publisher
SanFrancisco
www.INTERSTARNET.llc